THE BLACKPRINT

Proven Laws for Success

J. Michael Sherman

The Catalyst Global Network, LLC

INTRODUCTION

The Blueprint Beneath Our Feet

On July 25, 1946, Irene Morgan stood her ground on a Greyhound bus in Virginia, refusing to give up her seat nearly a decade before Rosa Parks' famous act of defiance. Dragged off the bus, arrested, and fined, Morgan took her case all the way to the U.S. Supreme Court—and won. Her victory in Morgan v. Virginia struck down segregation on interstate buses, yet her story remains overshadowed in the broader narrative of civil rights. This is the reality for many Black pioneers: innovators, thinkers, and leaders whose contributions laid the foundation for the freedoms we fight for today but whose names remain unwritten in history books. The Blackprint exists to honor these unsung heroes and to chart a course for the revolutionaries of tomorrow.

Black history isn't a sidebar to American history, It is foundational to American History. From the ingenuity of inventors to the resilience of civil rights leaders, Black contributions have shaped every corner of this nation. Yet, these stories are too often confined to a month of remembrance, rather than woven into the very fabric of our shared history.

This book is both a tribute and a challenge. It honors

the trailblazers who carved paths through oppression, illuminating the power of the African diaspora. But it also calls on us, the inheritors of this legacy, to rise, fight, and build upon the foundations they laid. The spirit of innovation, resistance, and excellence that fueled their journeys lives on in us.

The Blackprint is more than a collection of historical facts. It is a roadmap, a guide to understanding how the past informs our present and how it can empower us to shape the future. Each chapter reflects the greatness embedded in Black history and offers a call to action for all marginalized communities to reclaim their power and join the ongoing revolution.

This is our story. This is The Blackprint.

CHAPTER ONE

ARCHITECTS OF INNOVATION

From the earliest days of this nation, Black innovators have shaped the course of American history. Despite the barriers of systemic racism and limited access to resources, their contributions have fueled progress and transformed industries. This chapter explores the brilliance and resilience of Black inventors, scientists, and entrepreneurs who dared to dream beyond the constraints imposed upon them.

Granville T. Woods, often referred to as the "Black Edison," revolutionized the railway system with over 60 patents, including the multiplex telegraph, which allowed communication between moving trains and stations. His inventions not only enhanced transportation safety but also laid the groundwork for future technological advancements.

Madam C.J. Walker was the first self-made female millionaire in America, building an empire from her innovative haircare products designed specifically for Black women. Her business acumen and philanthropic efforts created opportunities for thousands of Black entrepreneurs and empowered women to embrace their beauty and potential.

George Washington Carver, born into slavery, became one of the most prominent scientists of his time. His agricultural research and promotion of crop rotation transformed farming in the South, and his work with peanuts and sweet potatoes created sustainable agricultural practices that benefited generations of farmers.

> *"I, wisdom, dwell with prudence, and find out knowledge of witty inventions." Proverbs 8:12*

The ingenuity displayed by Black inventors is a testament to the wisdom and resilience embedded in our heritage. Their work is not just a reflection of personal achievement but a contribution to the collective advancement of humanity.

Innovation has always been a form of resistance. In a society that sought to suppress Black potential, these pioneers forged new paths, proving that brilliance knows no racial boundaries. Their inventions were not just technical achievements, they were declarations of existence, proof that Black minds could and would shape the future.

Today, we find ourselves in a new era of opportunity for innovation. The current debate over H-1B visas in the United States highlights the growing demand for specialized talent in technology, engineering, and other fields. Companies are increasingly seeking foreign talent to fill critical roles, signaling a gap in local innovation and problem-solving. This is a pivotal time for atypical businesses and out-of-the-box thinkers to step up. Whether it's developing tech solutions for underserved communities, creating sustainable products that address environmental issues, or launching platforms that bridge gaps in education and healthcare, the opportunities are endless.

For those holding back out of fear that their ideas are too unconventional—this is your moment. History has shown us that it takes boldness and courage to see problems and bring solutions. Those who dare to challenge the norm and offer creative, impactful solutions are often the highest-paid and most successful, regardless of economic conditions. The marketplace rewards problem-solvers, and now more than ever, the world is looking for fresh perspectives and innovative ideas.

If Granville T. Woods had been afraid to challenge existing technologies, or if Madam C.J. Walker had doubted the viability of her products, we wouldn't be celebrating their legacies today. Your idea, no matter how unconventional, could be the next breakthrough that transforms industries and communities.

Modern Innovators Continuing the Legacy: Today, Black innovators continue to break barriers in fields ranging from technology to medicine. Dr. Kizzmekia Corbett, a leading scientist behind the development of the

COVID-19 vaccine, exemplifies how Black excellence in science continues to save lives and shape global health. Entrepreneurs like Tristan Walker, founder of Bevel, have created products that address the unique needs of the Black community while challenging traditional business models.

The legacy of Black innovation is a powerful reminder that creativity, resilience, and brilliance are woven into the fabric of our identity. By celebrating these contributions, we inspire future generations to pursue their dreams, knowing that they stand on the shoulders of giants.

Reflective Thought: Innovation is not just about creating something new, it's about daring to imagine beyond limitations. As we reflect on these trailblazers, ask yourself: What barriers can I break? Where can I innovate in my own life and community to build a legacy of change?

CHAPTER TWO

INTELLECTUAL GIANTS AND THE POWER OF THOUGHT

The pen has always been mightier than the sword, and throughout history, Black intellectuals have wielded it to challenge oppression, reshape narratives, and inspire revolutions. From the early scholars who navigated the turbulent waters of post-slavery America to modern thinkers redefining what it means to be Black in the 21st century, the power of thought has been a driving force in our collective journey.

W.E.B. Du Bois, the first African American to earn a Ph.D. from Harvard University, was a towering figure in sociology and civil rights advocacy. His seminal work, The Souls of Black Folk, introduced the concept of "double consciousness," describing the internal conflict experienced by subordinated groups in an oppressive society. Du Bois's intellectual rigor laid the groundwork for future civil rights movements and academic inquiry into race and identity.

Carter G. Woodson, known as the "Father of Black History," established Negro History Week in 1926, which later evolved into Black History Month. His groundbreaking book, The Mis-Education of the Negro, critiqued the education system for its failure to properly represent Black history and contributions. Woodson's work emphasized the importance of self-knowledge and cultural pride as tools for empowerment.

Frances Cress Welsing, a psychiatrist and author of The Isis Papers, provided provocative analyses on the psychological impact of racism. Her work delved into the intersections of race, culture, and power, challenging both academic and societal norms about race relations in America.

The intellectual tradition among Black thinkers has always been met with resistance. Whether through systemic exclusion from academic institutions, targeted discrediting of their work, or the outright erasure of their contributions, Black intellectuals have had to fight for their place in history. The attacks were not merely academic; they were deeply personal, designed to undermine credibility and silence voices that challenged the status quo. Yet, their resilience and brilliance have not only carved out spaces in academia but have also reshaped global perspectives on race, justice, and humanity.

Frances Cress Welsing's Vision for Empowerment: Dr. Welsing didn't just diagnose the psychological wounds inflicted by racism; she offered a blueprint for healing and empowerment. She urged the Black community to invest in self-knowledge, cultural pride, and economic independence. Welsing advocated for the strengthening of Black family units, the promotion of healthy lifestyles, and the nurturing of young minds to resist the psychological warfare waged by systemic racism. Her plan emphasized education—not just formal education, but the continuous learning of Black history, culture, and identity as a form of resistance and empowerment.

One of the most remarkable, yet often overlooked, contributions to the preservation of truth comes from Marion Stokes, a former librarian and activist who recorded 35 years of uninterrupted television news—from 1977 until her death in 2012. Stokes understood the power of media in shaping public perception and was determined to create an unalterable record of history as it unfolded. Her commitment wasn't just archival; it was an act of intellectual resistance. In an age where information could be manipulated or forgotten, Stokes ensured that future generations would have access to unfiltered truth. Her archive, now housed at the Internet Archive, serves as a critical resource for understanding media bias, historical revisionism, and the evolution of public discourse.

Stokes' work reflects the intellectual rigor and foresight that many Black thinkers have embodied throughout history. It's a reminder that the battle for truth isn't only fought in academia or public forums—it happens in quiet, persistent acts of preservation. Without individuals like Stokes, entire chapters of history risk being lost or distorted. Her work underscores the need for our generation of scholars and activists to take up the mantle, ensuring that the stories and truths of marginalized communities are preserved, honored, and built upon.

My own journey as a student was profoundly shaped by

my mentor, Dr. Donald Chinula, during my undergraduate studies at Stillman College. Sitting in his classroom, I was introduced to many of the thinkers mentioned in this chapter. Dr. Chinula's work, Building King's Beloved Community, opened my eyes to the power of faith and intellectualism in the fight for justice. Without his guidance and challenge, I would not have developed such a deep appreciation for the richness of Black thought. His influence on my academic and spiritual journey is a testament to the transformative power of mentorship and intellectual engagement.

The battle for intellectual freedom is ongoing. As new data and perspectives emerge, the legacies of many pioneering Black intellectuals face scrutiny and, at times, unjust criticism. While academic rigor demands that we continuously evaluate and question ideas, it is equally vital to honor the context and courage it took for these thinkers to challenge the status quo in their time. Their works were not just academic contributions, they were acts of defiance against systemic oppression and intellectual erasure.

Our generation of scholars carry the responsibility to build on what our predecessors have done. If we neglect their groundbreaking ideas, failing to engage with or expand upon them, we risk allowing their thoughts and contributions to fade into oblivion. This isn't merely about preserving history; it's about recognizing that the foundation they laid is essential for the progress we seek today. Their theories, writings, and activism serve as blueprints for new solutions to ongoing struggles.

My aim with works like The Blackprint is to honor my mentors and the ancestors who gave so much to empower the next generation of thinkers. Through studying and expanding their work, we continue the legacy of intellectual resilience and ensure that their voices echo in the halls of academia and beyond. The revolution of thought is as critical as any march or protest—it is the foundation upon which sustainable change is built.

CHAPTER THREE

JUSTICE AS A SACRED CALL

Justice has always been more than a legal principle for the Black community, it is a sacred calling. The fight for justice, from the abolition of slavery to the modern-day Black Lives Matter movement, is deeply rooted in the spiritual and moral conviction that all people are created equal and deserve dignity. This chapter explores the legacy of Black leaders who have fought for justice and the evolving challenges and criticisms faced by modern movements.

Fannie Lou Hamer famously declared, "I'm sick and tired of being sick and tired." As a civil rights leader and co-founder of the Mississippi Freedom Democratic Party, Hamer's fight for voting rights in the face of systemic disenfranchisement reflected the broader struggle for political justice. Her unwavering faith and courage in the face of violence and intimidation highlights how the pursuit of justice is often intertwined with personal sacrifice.

Thurgood Marshall, the first African American Supreme Court Justice, played a pivotal role in dismantling institutionalized segregation through landmark cases like Brown v. Board of Education. His legal brilliance and dedication to civil rights law set a precedent for future generations of Black lawyers and activists.

However, the modern fight for justice faces unique challenges. Movements like Black Lives Matter have been criticized for their broad inclusion of issues beyond race, such as LGBTQ+ rights and gender equality. Some argue that these alliances dilute the focus on racial justice, while others see them as essential components of an intersectional approach to oppression. This tension highlights the complexity of modern activism, where multiple identities and issues intersect in the fight for equality.

Popular narratives often suggest that movements have become too fragmented, but history tells us that solidarity across different struggles strengthens the fight for justice. The civil rights movement of the 1960s was not just about race, it was about economic justice, gender equality, and peace. Leaders like Bayard Rustin, a key organizer of the March on Washington, were openly gay and instrumental in shaping the movement's direction.

The critique that these movements are divisive overlooks the reality that Black people are not monolithic. Our struggles and identities are diverse, and our liberation must encompass all facets of who we are. The notion that fighting for Black justice should be separate from other forms of oppression fails to recognize the interconnectedness of these struggles.

Modern Advocates for Justice: Today, leaders like Bryan Stevenson, founder of the Equal Justice Initiative, continue the fight against systemic racism in the criminal justice system. Stevenson's work, chronicled in Just Mercy, exposes the deep racial biases that persist in American law. Patrisse Cullors, co-founder of Black Lives Matter, has expanded the conversation around justice to include a broader spectrum of marginalized voices, advocating for a more inclusive and holistic approach to activism.

My own journey as a pastor and counselor reflects the multifaceted nature of justice. I use my voice to challenge not just legal and economic systems but also the spiritual and psychological barriers that oppress our communities. Justice isn't confined to the courtroom, it's in our homes, our schools, our churches, and our hearts. Through my ministry and advocacy, I strive to create spaces where people can heal, grow, and reclaim their dignity.

Justice is not a destination. Justice is a continuous journey with many opportunites for growth along the way. From ancient civilizations to modern societies, justice has served as the cornerstone of moral and social order. The Law Code of Hammurabi, one of the oldest deciphered writings of significant length, set forth a comprehensive system of laws aimed at establishing fairness and accountability within the Babylonian empire. These laws were designed to protect the vulnerable and maintain social stability, reflecting the belief that justice was integral to a prosperous society.

Similarly, the Ten Commandments provided a moral framework that influenced not only religious communities but also the development of Western legal systems. These commandments emphasize principles of honesty, respect, and compassion—values essential for the flourishing of any civilization. The moral implications of these ancient laws underscore the universal need for justice as a foundation for societal success.

However, when we contrast these ideals with the current state of justice in the United States, a troubling picture emerges. The very principles that once guided the nation toward greater equality and civil rights are now under threat. The current administration has overseen policies that roll back key civil rights era legislation, and the Supreme Court's decision to deem affirmative action unlawful marks a significant regression in the fight for educational and economic equity. Furthermore, Diversity, Equity, and Inclusion (DEI) initiatives, once celebrated for fostering inclusive environments, are now vilified in public discourse, treated as divisive rather than unifying principles.

The threat doesn't stop there. In Mississippi, a proposed law eerily reminiscent of the Fugitive Slave Act aims to increase state control over local law enforcement, potentially targeting marginalized communities with discriminatory practices. This law, if passed, could set a dangerous precedent, signaling a broader erosion of civil rights protections across the nation. History has shown us that when one group is deemed "less than," the repercussions can extend to any marginalized community.

These developments are not abstract political issues, they have real, tangible impacts on the lives of millions. They are a stark reminder that justice is fragile and must be actively defended. We cannot afford to be passive observers in this struggle. The moral and legal frameworks that once propelled societies toward justice must now be invoked to counter these regressive forces.

Our involvement in justice must be proactive and relentless. Whether through legal advocacy, community organizing, or standing up against discriminatory policies, each of us has a role to play. Justice is not a relic of the past, it is a living, breathing pursuit that demands our engagement in real time. The stakes are too high, and the cost of inaction is far too great.

As we honor the legacy of those who have fought before us, we must ask ourselves: How will we join the fight for justice today? Whether through legal advocacy, community organizing, or simply standing up for what is right in our daily lives, each of us has a role to play in this sacred call.

CHAPTER FOUR

BUILDING BLACK WEALTH AND ECONOMIC EMPOWERMENT

Black wealth has never just been about money. For generations, it's been a symbol of freedom, resilience, and legacy—a testament to our ability to thrive in a system that was never designed for us to succeed. We've faced obstacles that would have broken other communities: redlining, discriminatory lending, being excluded from critical policies like the GI Bill and New Deal. And yet, here we are—still building, still thriving, still creating paths where none existed.

But the conversation about Black wealth isn't just historical—it's personal. It's about the decisions we make today, the communities we invest in, and the legacies we leave behind. We've been dealt an unfair hand, but we're still at the table. Now, it's time to play to win.

Understanding the Historical Context

To understand where we're going, we have to be honest about where we've been. Before the New Deal, Black families were systematically excluded from key economic opportunities like homeownership and Social Security benefits. The policies that lifted millions of Americans into the middle class left us behind, reinforcing cycles of poverty and exclusion.

Take the GI Bill, for example, a transformative policy that helped returning veterans buy homes and pursue higher education. But for Black veterans, this promise was hollow. Local discriminatory practices ensured that many were denied access to these benefits, pushing them into menial jobs and substandard housing while their white counterparts-built wealth that would be passed down for generations.

These policies didn't just slow us down, they created an economic divide that we're still trying to bridge today. According to a 2019 Brookings report, the median white household has a net worth of $171,000, compared to $17,150 for Black households—about ten times greater. Black families own about 2.6% of the nation's wealth, despite making up 13% of the population. Homeownership rates also reflect this disparity: 72% of white families own homes compared to 42% of Black families.

Acknowledging this history isn't about dwelling on the past. It's about understanding the systemic forces at play so we can strategize for the future. Because the truth is, we've always found a way to thrive, no matter what the odds.

Pioneers of Black Economic Empowerment

Throughout history, there have been trailblazers who refused to accept the limits imposed on them. They didn't wait for permission to succeed—they created their own opportunities and uplifted their communities in the process.

Madam C.J. Walker is a name we all know, but her story never gets old. She wasn't just the first female self-made millionaire in America; she was a visionary entrepreneur who built an empire from the ground up, providing jobs and economic opportunities for countless Black women. Her legacy isn't just about wealth, it's about empowerment.

Then there's A.G. Gaston, a businessman who defied segregation and economic exclusion in the South to build a financial empire. He didn't just accumulate wealth for himself, he created opportunities for others through employment, financial services, and education. Gaston understood that true wealth isn't just personal, it's communal.

And we can't forget Reginald Lewis, the first African American to build a billion-dollar company. His work with TLC Beatrice International shattered stereotypes and proved that Black entrepreneurs could succeed on a global stage.

These pioneers didn't just survive, they thrived. They built blueprints that we can follow today, adapting their strategies to our modern world.

Wealth Today: The Blueprint

So, what does building Black wealth look like in today's world? It's not just about individual successes. We must create systems of support, circulating wealth within our communities, and laying the groundwork for generational prosperity.

1. Financial Literacy: Knowledge is Power

You can't build wealth without understanding how money works. Budgeting, saving, investing, and credit management are the cornerstones of financial stability. But for too long, this knowledge has been kept out of reach for many in our community.

Community-led financial literacy programs are key. It's one thing to learn these skills individually, but when entire communities are empowered with financial knowledge, the impact is transformative. We need to make financial education as common in our communities as Sunday service.

2. Investing in Black-Owned Businesses

Every dollar we spend is a vote for the kind of economy and community we want to build. When we support Black-owned businesses, we're not just buying a product, we're investing in economic growth and job creation within our communities.

Look at entrepreneurs like Daymond John, founder of FUBU, who turned a small clothing line into a cultural phenomenon. Or Richelieu Dennis, the mastermind behind SheaMoisture, who built his brand while staying true to his roots and giving back to his community. These modern pioneers show us that supporting Black businesses isn't just an act of solidarity, it's an investment in our collective future.

3. Real Estate: Ownership is Liberation

Homeownership remains one of the most powerful tools for building generational wealth. But let's be real, this hasn't always been an accessible path for us. Redlining may be illegal today, but its effects linger, and many Black families still face hurdles when it comes to securing loans and buying property.

But that doesn't mean the door is closed. Programs offering down payment assistance and financial counseling can help bridge the gap, but we also need to be proactive in seeking out these opportunities. Ownership is about power. And the more we own, the more control we have over our futures.

4. Entrepreneurship and Innovation: Creating Our Own Opportunities

Black entrepreneurs have always been at the forefront of innovation. From Madam C.J. Walker's haircare empire to today's tech startups, we've proven that we can create solutions to problems the world didn't even know existed.

But entrepreneurship isn't just about starting a business. We have to use business to create economic independence. We need more mentorship programs to support aspiring entrepreneurs and greater access to venture capital for Black-owned startups. The future of Black wealth is in our ideas, and it's time to bring those ideas to life.

5. Estate Planning: Protecting What We Build

Building wealth is one thing, but preserving it is just as important. Too often, families lose hard-earned wealth because they don't have a plan for transferring it across generations.

Wills, trusts, and other estate planning tools are essential for ensuring that wealth isn't lost but passed down. This isn't just about money. We have to secure a future for our children and their children. Legacy is the ultimate form of wealth.

6. Strengthening Black Families: The Heart of Economic Empowerment

Economic empowerment is deeply connected to the strength of our families. Strong family units provide the foundation for financial stability and community resilience. Frances Cress Welsing spoke about the importance of family cohesion in the fight against systemic oppression. When families are united, they create a powerful support system that nurtures both emotional and financial well-being.

Challenges and Triumphs

Yes, we've faced challenges, some of them unimaginable. But we've also made incredible progress. From the rise of Black billionaires like Oprah Winfrey and Robert F. Smith to the thriving local businesses in our own neighborhoods, the narrative of Black wealth isn't just one of struggle, it's one of triumph, innovation, and perseverance. It's time for massive action.

The journey toward economic empowerment isn't about individual success, it's about lifting entire communities. The blueprint is here. Now, it's up to us to act. Start Small, Think Big: Support a local Black-owned business, set up a savings plan, mentor a young entrepreneur. Every step matters.

What will you do today to contribute to the economic empowerment of your family and community?

> *"Money can't talk, but it can make lies look true." - African Proverb.*

Let's ensure our wealth tells the truth of our resilience, creativity, and unbreakable spirit.

CHAPTER FIVE

RECLAIMING OUR CULTURAL LEGACY

From the spirituals sung by enslaved Africans in the fields to the Harlem Renaissance poets who redefined Black identity, art has always been at the heart of our liberation. Figures like Langston Hughes, whose poetry captured both the pain and beauty of the Black experience, and Zora Neale Hurston, who chronicled the richness of Black folklore, used their voices to challenge the dominant narratives of their time. Their work wasn't just about self-expression, it was about cultural reclamation and empowerment.

In the realm of visual art, Aaron Douglas used his paintings to connect African heritage with contemporary Black life, while Augusta Savage sculpted the struggles and triumphs of her people into tangible form. In music, Ma Rainey, the "Mother of the Blues," laid the foundation for genres that would become the backbone of American music, influencing generations of artists.

These pioneers understood that art is more than entertainment, it's a powerful tool for resistance and cultural preservation. Their creativity laid the groundwork for today's artists, who continue to navigate the complex intersection of art, commerce, and identity.

Reclaiming our cultural legacy is not just about remembering the past, it's about actively shaping the narrative of the present and future. Throughout history, Black culture has been a cornerstone of American music, art, and literature, but it has often been misappropriated, commodified, or dismissed. Now more than ever, we are witnessing a powerful resurgence of Black cultural reclamation efforts that aim to restore authenticity, ownership, and pride.

Musical Reclamation

The music industry has long profited from Black creativity while marginalizing Black artists. Recent events, such as the public scrutiny of industry moguls like Sean "P. Diddy" Combs, highlight the systemic issues within the industry that exploit Black talent. Simultaneously, artists like Beyoncé are reclaiming the narratives, with projects like Black Is King celebrating African heritage and culture on a global scale. The rise of independent Black artists leveraging digital platforms to retain creative control and financial ownership is a testament to this shift.

Recently, the popularity of artists like Sexyy Red has sparked debates within the Black community about the narratives being sold and the broader implications for cultural representation. While artistic expression is diverse and valid, the commercial promotion of certain stereotypes raises critical questions about who controls the cultural narrative and for what purpose.

Gospel music has always been a bedrock of Black cultural expression, offering both spiritual uplift and a voice of resistance. Contemporary artists like Kirk Franklin and Maverick City Music are blending traditional gospel with modern sounds, reaching new audiences while staying rooted in faith and cultural heritage. This fusion not only keeps gospel music relevant but also underscores its role in the broader tapestry of Black cultural reclamation.

Culutural Reclamation

Initiatives like the #BlackLivesMatter murals painted across major cities, the resurgence of African fashion in global runways, and the celebration of Juneteenth as a national holiday reflect the ways Black culture is being reclaimed and recognized. These efforts are more than symbolic; they represent a collective assertion of identity and history that resists erasure and misrepresentation.

These reclamation efforts foster a sense of pride, unity, and empowerment within the Black community. They challenge the dominant narratives that have historically marginalized Black voices and offer a more authentic and diverse portrayal of Black life and culture. By reclaiming our cultural legacy, we not only honor our ancestors but also inspire future generations to embrace their heritage unapologetically.

Reclaiming our cultural legacy is a continuous journey. It requires vigilance, creativity, and a collective commitment to ensure that our stories are told, our contributions are acknowledged, and our culture is celebrated on our own terms.

CHAPTER SIX

THE BLACK FAITH LEADERS WHO SHAPED OUR SPIRIT

Faith within the Black community has always been more than a set of beliefs, it has been a dynamic force of resistance, resilience, and revolution. From the plantation fields to the pulpit, from the mosques to the march lines, spirituality has been the backbone of our struggle and the blueprint for our liberation. But as we honor the legacy of Black faith, we must also confront how its power has been misused and diluted, particularly by those who have allowed politics and personal gain to overshadow true community transformation.

Christian Contributions: Faith as a Catalyst for Justice

The influence of Christian leaders like Dr. Martin Luther King Jr. and Sojourner Truth is undeniable. Their ability to intertwine faith with the call for justice created movements that didn't just change laws, they redefined the soul of America. Churches became sanctuaries for organizing, resistance, and healing, demonstrating the powerful intersection of spirituality and activism. The pulpit was not just a place for sermons, it was a platform for revolution.

But the story doesn't start with King. Frederick Douglass, born into slavery, found his first taste of freedom through the pages of the Bible. Taught to read by his slave master's wife and later teaching himself to read the scriptures, Douglass discovered not just spiritual enlightenment but intellectual liberation. He didn't hoard this knowledge—he shared with others, empowering enslaved people with the tools to read, think, and fight for their own freedom.

Douglass later criticized the hypocrisy of slaveholders who used Christianity to justify oppression, declaring, "Between the Christianity of this land and the Christianity of Christ, I recognize the widest possible difference." This boldness is a reminder that faith must always stand on the side of justice, not oppression.

Muslim Contributions: A Revolution of the Mind and Spirit

While the Black church has been a cornerstone, the Muslim faith has also played a pivotal role in empowering Black communities. The Nation of Islam and leaders like El-Hajj Malik El-Shabazz (Malcolm X) redefined Black identity, promoting self-determination, economic self-sufficiency, and pride in our heritage. Malcolm's fiery speeches weren't just about confronting racism—they were about confronting the internalized narratives of inferiority and powerlessness that had been forced upon us.

Later, Warith Deen Mohammed took a transformative step by leading many in the Nation of Islam toward orthodox Sunni Islam, emphasizing the universal principles of justice while maintaining a strong commitment to addressing the unique struggles of Black Americans. His leadership showed that faith can evolve without losing its revolutionary edge.

African Spiritual Traditions: Reclaiming Our Roots

Before Christianity and Islam, we were a people rich in spiritual traditions deeply connected to the land, ancestors, and the cosmos. Traditions like Yoruba, Vodun, and Ifá were not just religious systems—they were ways of life that emphasized community, balance, and respect for the natural world.

The forced erasure of these traditions during slavery was a deliberate attempt to disconnect us from our heritage. But they never truly died. Today, the revival and reclamation of African spirituality affirm our cultural heritage and provide spiritual grounding in modern struggles for justice. These practices remind us that we are more than the sum of our oppressions—we are the descendants of kings, queens, and spiritual leaders who understood the sacredness of community and the power of the unseen.

Contemporary Faith Leaders: The State of Black Leadership Today

In modern times, leaders like Bishop Yvette Flunder and Rev. Dr. William Barber II continue the legacy of faith-driven activism. Flunder challenges both religious and societal norms by advocating for inclusivity within the church, while Barber has reignited the Poor People's Campaign, demanding justice for the marginalized.

However, we must be honest about the state of Black leadership today. Too many faith leaders have become entangled in politics, prioritizing visibility and influence over real community change. Some have used the pulpit not to uplift, but to exploit. They have turned sacred spaces into platforms for personal gain while their communities suffer.

Religion, in too many cases, has been weaponized and used to control rather than liberate. The same Bible that once taught Frederick Douglass to read and resist has been twisted by some to justify greed, misogyny, and oppression within our own communities. It's time to reclaim our faith, not as a tool of compliance but as a force for transformation.

Reclaiming Spiritual Authority: A Call to Black Biblical Scholars

The future of Black faith lies not just in preserving traditional practices, but in evolving them to meet today's challenges. We need more Black biblical scholars, theologians, and spiritual leaders who can provide fresh interpretations that speak to the lived experiences of our communities.

This isn't just about the church, it's about reclaiming our spiritual authority across all faith traditions. Whether through Christianity, Islam, or African spirituality, the goal remains the same: to use our faith as a weapon against injustice, a healing balm for our communities, and a guide toward liberation.

A Critical Reflection

Our ancestors understood the power of faith. They used it to break chains, both literal and figurative. But faith without action is hollow. And action without integrity is dangerous. As we move forward, we must ensure that our spiritual leaders are not just preaching change, they're living it.

Are we using our faith to liberate or to control?

Are we leading with love and justice, or with ego and greed?

Are we building communities that reflect the best of our traditions, or are we repeating the mistakes of those who once oppressed us?

The Blueprint for Spiritual Liberation

The future of Black faith isn't just about holding onto tradition, it's about transforming it. It's about creating spaces where faith and activism aren't separate, where spirituality is the foundation for community empowerment, and where our leaders are accountable to the people they serve.

Let's reclaim our faith,not as a relic of the past, but as a living, breathing force that propels us toward a future of justice, healing, and liberation.

CHAPTER SEVEN

RESTORING THE BLACK FAMILY, BREAKING THE CHAINS OF GENERATIONAL TRAUMA

We cannot talk about revolution without addressing the foundation of our communitiesthe family. The decline in marriage rates, the rise in single-parent households, and the fragmentation of family structures are not isolated issues. They are the byproducts of systemic oppression, historical trauma, and deliberate efforts to dismantle Black unity.

In 1960, 61% of Black adults were married. By 2008, that number dropped to 32%, compared to 56% of white adults. (Pew Research) Around 64% of Black children grow up in single-parent households, compared to 24% of white children. (U.S. Census Data) Black women experience higher divorce rates than any other group in the U.S. (National Library of Medicine)

These numbers tell a story of a people under siege. We're not speaking economically or politically, but spiritually and emotionally.

While economist Thomas Sowell argues that the welfare state of the New Deal played a central role in the decline of the Black family, I believe the roots of this issue run deeper, tied not just to policy but to psychological manipulation. The welfare system may have contributed to economic instability, but it operated within a broader historical framework designed to fracture Black unity. This blueprint for division mirrors the strategies outlined in the infamous Willie Lynch Letter—a document that, though widely believed to be a hoax, reflects very real tactics used to control and destabilize enslaved people and their descendants.

The Willie Lynch Letter describes a methodical plan to sow division within the Black community by pitting the young against the old, the light-skinned against the dark-skinned, and most devastatingly, the man against the woman. While its historical authenticity is disputed, the psychological strategies it details resonate deeply because they reflect actual practices that were used to maintain control over Black people. During slavery, families were systematically torn apart. Husbands were sold away from wives, children were ripped from their mothers' arms, and generations were left to cope with the trauma of familial separation. This wasn't just about physical division, it was about creating psychological dependency, mistrust, and fragmentation.

Even after emancipation, Jim Crow laws, mass incarceration, and economic disenfranchisement continued to destabilize Black families.

By understanding the interplay between economic

disenfranchisement and psychological manipulation, we can begin to dismantle the systems that were designed to divide us and reclaim the strength of our families.

Frances Cress Welsing argued that racism isn't just about discrimination. Racism is a system of power. She suggests that it is based in a very real fear of genetic annelation. Furthermore, she states that racist system is designed to keep the white minority as the ruling class although the vast majority of the world is made of people of color. She warned us, that racism would not dissapea and said efforts to undermine the Black identity, unity, and family structures would persist. She emphasized that the restoration of the Black family is central to resisting systemic oppression.

When families break, the ripple effects are felt throughout the community.

1. Economic Impact:

Single-parent households face more significant economic challenges, limiting wealth-building opportunities and perpetuating the racial wealth gap.

2. Educational Outcomes:

Children from two-parent households statistically perform better in school and have greater access to resources. However, this isn't a reflection of capability, it's a reflection of systemic barriers.

3. Mental Health and Emotional Stability:

The breakdown of family structures leads to increased trauma, identity struggles, and difficulties forming healthy relationships.

"God sets the lonely in families." Psalm 68:6

The Path Forward: Restoring What Was Broken

We carry the pain, the anger, and the frustration of generations. But pain is not the end of our story, it's the fuel for our revolution.

We cannot wait for perfect conditions to begin restoring our families. We must start where we are, with what we have, and with who we are.

A. For the Single Man

1. Embrace Responsibility:

You don't have to wait until you have a family to be a father figure. Mentor young men in your community, support your nieces and nephews, and be present in the lives of others.

2. Heal from Trauma:

Seek counseling or support to address unresolved pain

from absent fathers or broken relationships. Healing yourself is the first step to breaking generational cycles.

3. Build Partnerships:

Cultivate healthy relationships, whether romantic or platonic, that encourage emotional vulnerability and growth.

Jawanza Kunjufu, in his seminal work Countering the Conspiracy to Destroy Black Boys, emphasized the importance of strong male role models and family involvement in the development of Black boys. He identified how systemic structures, like the educational system and mass incarceration, aim to undermine Black manhood and destabilize family units. His work serves as a call to action for men to step into mentorship and leadership roles within their families and communities.

B. For the Single Woman

1. Prioritize Self-Worth:

You are more than your relationship status. Invest in yourself—spiritually, emotionally, and financially.

2. Model Healthy Love:

Whether you have children or not, demonstrate what self-respect, resilience, and love look like in action.

3. Cultivate Community:

Build networks of support with other women who uplift and encourage you. Sisterhood is a powerful tool for healing and growth.

Bell hooks, in "Salvation: Black People and Love", argued that love is a political act in the face of oppression. She urged Black women to reclaim love, for themselves, their communities, and their families. She admonished Black women to use it as a revolutionary tool for healing and restoration.

C. Rebuilding the Family Unit

1. Communication is Key:

Hold regular family meetings. Talk openly about struggles and victories. Silence is the enemy of healing.

2. Lap Time (Dr. Welsing's Concept):

Physical closeness between parents and children fosters emotional security. Prioritize quality time. Remembereven small moments matter.

3. Financial Empowerment:

Teach financial literacy within the family. Discuss budgeting, saving, and building generational wealth.

4. Faith as Foundation:

Reconnect with your spiritual roots. Whether through church, meditation, or ancestral traditions, faith grounds us.

5. Cultural Reclamation:

Teach your children about their history, heritage, and the strength of their ancestors. Knowledge of self is a weapon against oppression.

The revolution begins at home. Restoring the Black family is the most radical act of resistance we can undertake. It is the foundation of our community, the cradle of our culture, and the blueprint for our future.

You may feel the weight of generations of pain, and that is valid. But do not let that pain paralyze you. Use it. Let it fuel your commitment to rebuild what was broken, to nurture what remains, and to plant seeds for the future.

> *"If you want to go fast, go alone. If you want to go far, go together."- African Proverb*

Start where you are. If you're estranged from a family member, make that call. If you've been absent from your children's lives, take that first step. If you feel isolated, build your community. The revolution doesn't start on the streets, it starts at home.

CONCLUSION

THE BLUEPRINT IS OURS TO BUILD

Throughout history, the Black community has faced barriers designed to limit our potential, diminish our power, and fragment our unity. But as we've seen in these pages, those barriers have never defined us. Instead, we've drawn from the well of innovation, intellectual prowess, economic resilience, spiritual strength, and now, the restoration of our families to craft something greater-a path forward that's uniquely ours.

From the bold entrepreneurship of Madam C.J. Walker to the intellectual trailblazing of W.E.B. Du Bois, from the fiery calls for justice by Malcolm X to the spiritual awakenings led by Frederick Douglass, our history is filled with examples of resistance and revolution. But beyond the grand movements and public figures, it's in the everyday choices, the decisions to invest in our communities, to uplift each other, to prioritize family. Thats where real revolution will take place.

In this journey, we've not only celebrated the architects of our past but laid out a master plan for the future. A plan that acknowledges our pain but refuses to be defined by it.

A plan that sees the power in our collective history and the promise of our shared future.

Restoring the Black family is the final, crucial piece of this blueprint. Our families are the bedrock of our strength, the foundation from which all other forms of empowerment flow. The attempts to fracture us, whether through systemic oppression, economic disenfranchisement, or psychological manipulation—were deliberate. But so is our response.

By healing our homes, we heal our communities. By investing in our relationships, we build unbreakable networks of support that ripple outward into society.

The journey toward success, as individuals, as families, and as a community, is not just about wealth or recognition. It's about wholeness. It's about honoring our ancestors by living fully into the futures they dreamed of but never saw. It's about reclaiming what was taken, restoring what was broken, and building what has yet to exist.

EPILOGUE

The Challenge Ahead

This isn't just a history book or a guide; it's a call to action. The Blackprint is our blueprint is here. The tools are in your hands. The stories of those who came before us have been told, but your story is still being written.

Will you innovate when the world tells you to conform?

Will you invest in your community when the system encourages isolation?

Will you nurture your family in a society designed to pull you apart?

Will you reclaim your spiritual authority when others misuse it for control?

The path won't always be easy. There will be setbacks, and there will be resistance. But remember: We have never been defined by the obstacles in our path. We are defined by how we rise, how we build, and how we come together to forge something new.

The Blackprint: Proven Laws for Success is more than just a reflection on our past, it's a living document for our future.

Every law, every principle, and every story shared in these chapters is a brick in the foundation of what's possible. However, the building isn't complete.

It's up to each of us to pick up where our ancestors left off and continue crafting a future worthy of their sacrifices and dreams.

We've inherited a rich history and a powerful legacy of greatness. Now, it's time to put that blueprint into action and build a future defined not by struggle, but by success, unity, and liberation.

The Blackprint is ours. Let's build.

ABOUT THE AUTHOR

J. Michael Sherman

J. Michael Sherman is a multifaceted pastor, counselor, and consultant dedicated to empowering communities through faith-based leadership, counseling, and business development. He leads Covenant Family Church in Augusta, Georgia, and founded The Catalyst Global Network, LLC, focusing on faith, family restoration, and financial growth.

Sherman holds a Bachelor's degree in Interdisciplinary Studies with concentrations in Behavioral and Social Sciences. He is currently pursuing a PhD in Human and Social Services, with integrated coursework leading to a Master's in Psychology. He has also completed advanced studies in Master of Divinity, blending theological insights with practical counseling approaches.

As a father and husband, Sherman's personal experiences fuel his passion for strengthening Black families and uplifting marginalized communities. In The Blackprint:

Proven Laws for Success, he highlights the overlooked contributions of Black innovators, intellectuals, and justice leaders, offering readers a master plan for economic empowerment and spiritual liberation.

BOOKS BY THIS AUTHOR

The Ministry Of Christ: Forgiveness And Oneness

Many well-meaning Christians get lost in dogmas, creeds, and politics of denominations, causing them to morph into religious police. This read is concise, biblically-focused, and hermeneutically sensitive. It's an encouraging devotional for the believer who is currently struggling with the shame of vices and character flaws. Additionally, it serves as a humble reminder to the mature Christian to lovingly extend the heart of Christ and help those who struggle in Christian communities to overcome evil with good.

Made in the USA
Columbia, SC
03 June 2025

58705019R00028